# How to Use MAPS

by Susan Ahmadi Hansen

PEBBLE
a capstone imprint

Published by Pebble, an imprint of Capstone
1710 Roe Crest Drive, North Mankato, Minnesota 56003
capstonepub.com

Library of Congress Cataloging-in-Publication Data is available on
the Library of Congress website.

ISBN: 9781666349658 (hardcover)
ISBN: 9781666349696 (paperback)
ISBN: 9781666349733 (ebook PDF)

Summary: How do maps work? What can they tell you? What do
all the lines and pictures mean? Discover how to use maps to get
information and find your way around!

Editorial Credits
Editor: Ericka Smith; Designer: Tracy Davies; Media Researcher:
Svetlana Zhurkin; Production Specialist: Katy LaVigne

Image Credits
Capstone: 11, Karon Dubke, 19, Maps.com, 10, Renée Doyle, 7;
Getty Images: Chachawal Prapai, 4; NOAA: Climate.gov/NDMC, 17;
Shutterstock: blinkblink (map), cover, 1, Kaspri, 11 (ruler), medejaja,
cover (hands), nataliya_ua, cover (compass rose), Olinchuk, 9,
overtheseas, 13, 15, Peter Hermes Furian, 5, Prostock-studio, 18,
Rainer Lesniewski, 21; XNR Productions: 16

Printed and bound in the USA.   4882

# TABLE OF CONTENTS

Words in **bold** are in the glossary.

## Maps and Their Uses

Have you ever used a map? Maybe you needed one to get around a park. Or maybe you used one to find a city in your state.

There are all kinds of maps. Maps teach us a lot about our world. How can you get to Chicago from Memphis? How far away is your state's capital?

# Finding Places

Need to find a place on a map? Look for the **key**. The key will tell you what different **symbols** mean. Symbols stand for different places.

Want to go for a swim? Find areas colored in blue. Looking for a big city near you? Find the nearest circle.

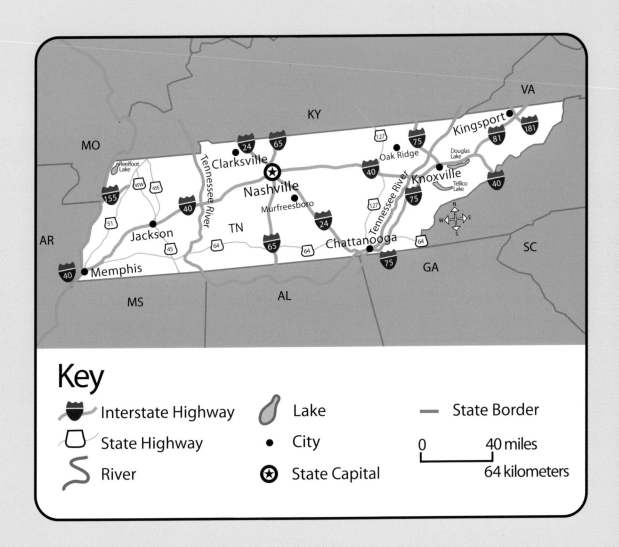

## Key

- 🛡 Interstate Highway
- ⬭ State Highway
- 〜 River
- ◖ Lake
- • City
- ✪ State Capital
- — State Border

0        40 miles

64 kilometers

## Using Grids

Some maps have **grids**. Grids are lines that form squares on a map. They are made of rows and columns.

Grids are labeled with letters and numbers. You use them to find a place on a map. For example, Jackson is in the square D7 on this map of Mississippi.

9

# Measuring Distances

Maps use **scales** to tell us what a distance is in real life. The scale might look like a ruler. The scale can also be written in words. Or it can be written as a fraction.

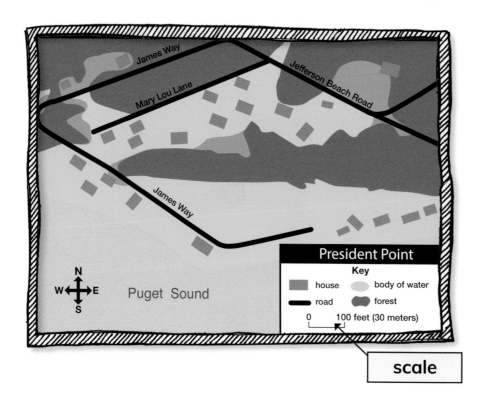

President Point

**Key**

- house
- body of water
- road
- forest

0    100 feet (30 meters)

scale

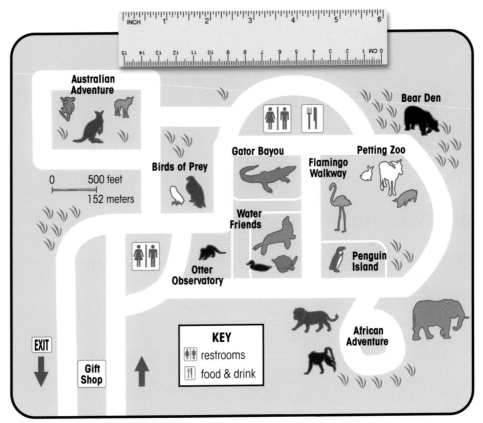

**Marksville Zoo**

Use a ruler to measure the distance between two places. Use the scale to find how far apart they really are.

## Using Cardinal Directions

We use maps to help us get somewhere. We might give directions using north (N), south (S), east (E), and west (W). These are **cardinal directions**. The letters on a **compass rose** show cardinal directions on a map.

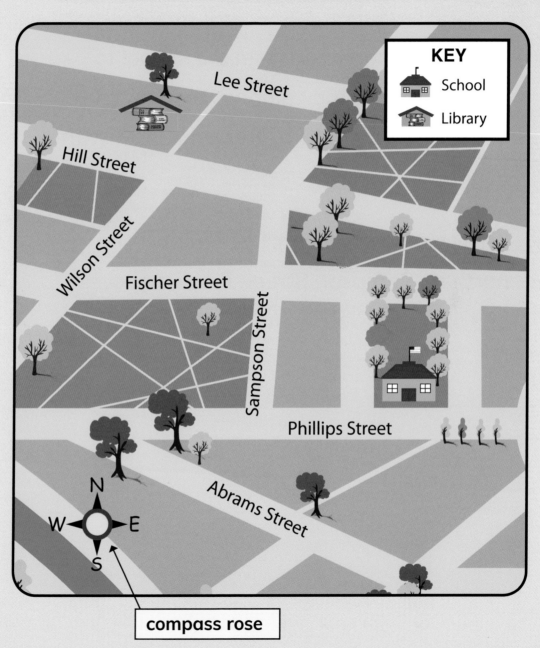

compass rose

Use this map to go from the school to the library. Use the compass rose to figure out which way to turn. Trace the path with your finger.

First, go west on Phillips Street. Then, go north on Sampson Street. Finally, go west on Hill Street. You've made it to the library.

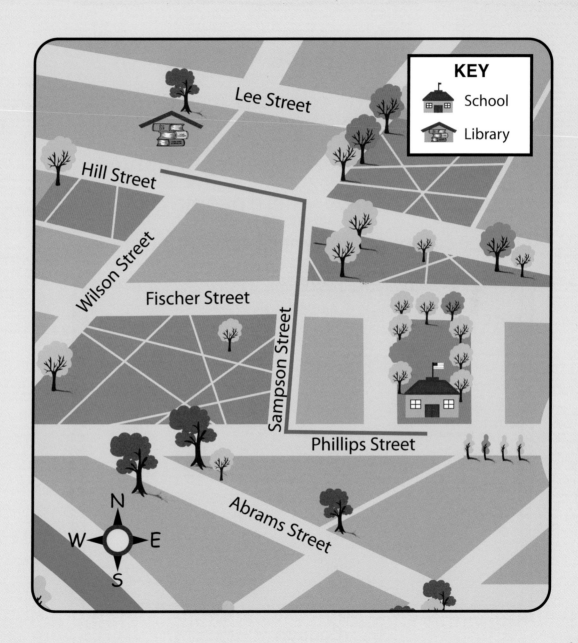

# Using Special Maps

Some maps show special information about a place. For example, a **population density** map shows where people live. Darker colors show where many people live.

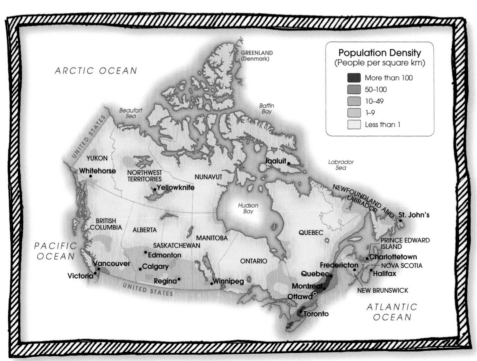

**Canada**

**Rain in the United States**

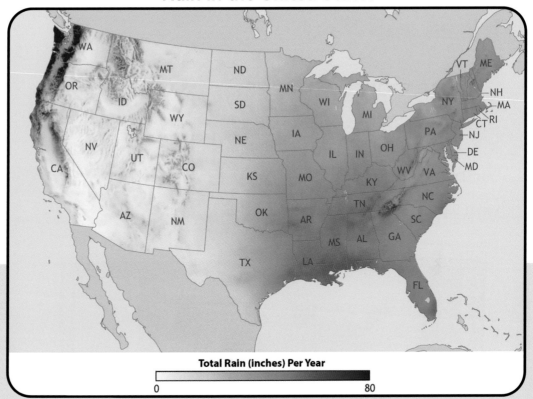

Total Rain (inches) Per Year

0    80

Climate maps show weather over time. A climate map might show how much rain usually falls in a year. Which places get a lot of rain? Which places get very little rain?

## Maps and You

Maps can answer many questions. Do you need to get somewhere? Do you want to learn about the weather in a place? Where's the playground at your school?

There are many types of maps. Each one can help you find the answers you need.

# Plan a Trip

Find a map of your state. Use it to plan a trip from your city to another place in the state. Follow these steps:

1. Use the grid to find your city.
2. Find another city you want to visit. (Use the grid to help you.)
3. Find highways and streets that connect the two places.
4. Use the scale to measure how far apart the two places are.
5. Use cardinal directions to write down the steps you'd take to get there. Here's an example: From Stevens Point, go south on Interstate 39 to Madison. Then go east on Interstate 94 until you get to Milwaukee.

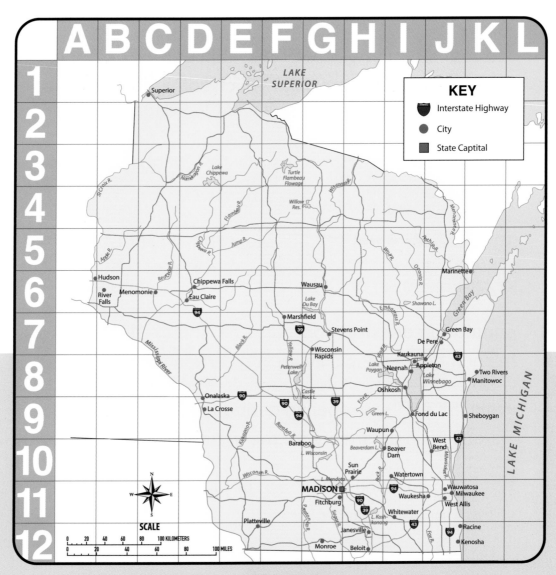

## Wisconsin

# Glossary

**cardinal directions** (KAHR-dih-nuhl duh-REK-shuhnz)—the four main points toward which something can face: north, south, east, and west

**compass rose** (KUHM-puhs ROHZ)—a label that shows direction on a map

**grid** (GRID)—a pattern of evenly spaced lines that cross

**key** (KEE)—a list or chart that explains symbols

**population density** (pop-yuh-LAY-shuhn DEN-sih-tee)—the number of people living in a certain amount of space

**scale** (SKALE)—a label on a map that compares the distances on the map with the actual distances on Earth

**symbol** (SIM-buhl)—a design or picture on a map that stands for something else

## Read More

Bell, Samantha. *The Purpose of Maps*. Mankato, MN: Child's World, 2019.

Hansen, Susan Ahmadi. *Types of Maps*. North Mankato, MN: Capstone, 2023.

Reed, Ellis M. *Compasses and Cardinal Directions*. Mankato, MN: Child's World, 2019.

## Internet Sites

*Britannica Kids: Map and Globe*
kids.britannica.com/kids/article/map-and-globe/353425

*National Geographic: What Is a Population Map?*
blog.education.nationalgeographic.org/2013/01/27/12298

*Wonderopolis: How Does a Compass Work?*
wonderopolis.org/wonder/how-does-a-compass-work

## Index

## About the Author

Susan Ahmadi Hansen is a children's writer and a teacher. She especially enjoys teaching young readers and writers to fall in love with books. Susan has four adult children who live on three different continents. She lives with her husband in Cedar Park, Texas.